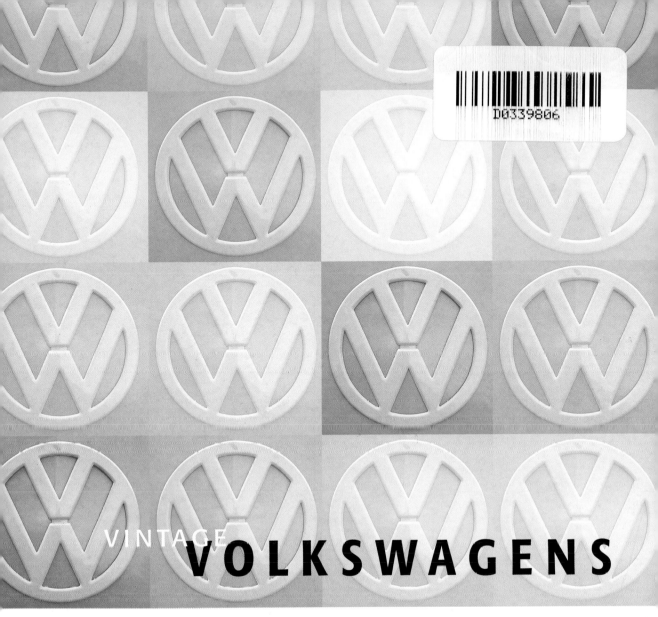

VINTAGE VOLKSWAGENS

Photography by > FLAT 4 PROJECT

CHRONICLE BOOKS

SAN FRANCISCO

This edition published in 1999 by Chronicle Books.

Printed in Hong Kong

Library of Congress Cataloging-in-Publication
Data available.

ISBN 0-8118-2545-0

Cover design: JEREMY STOUT
Cover photograph: FLAT 4 PROJECT

Distributed in Canada by
Raincoast Books
8680 Cambie Street
Vancouver, B.C. V6P 6M9

10 9 8 7 6 5 4 3 2 1

Chronicle Books
85 Second Street
San Francisco, California 94105

www.chroniclebooks.com

Introduction

In 1949, Volkswagen introduced a car that seemed to be the antithesis of American drivers' dreams. The Bug was small, funny looking, without frills and functional. America was postwar and prosperous. The Bug didn't make sense.

Yet it sold. As soon as there were Volkswagens, there were Volkswagen lovers. People who saw beauty in the Bug's new shape and value in its simple efficiency. Soon Bugs were dotting the American scene, carving a niche in the driving trends of the fifties. Then came the other VW's–the Karmann-Ghias, the Hebmullers, the buses and vans.

Now the Volkswagen seems like an idea that was ahead of its time. Vintage Volkswagens are finding their just place in the annals of automotive innovation.

A classic, according to Webster's dictionary, is "of the first or highest class or rank; serving as a standard, model or guide." What follows is a pictorial tribute to the unique design and timeless form of the Volkswagen greats— classics in the truest sense.

2

3

4

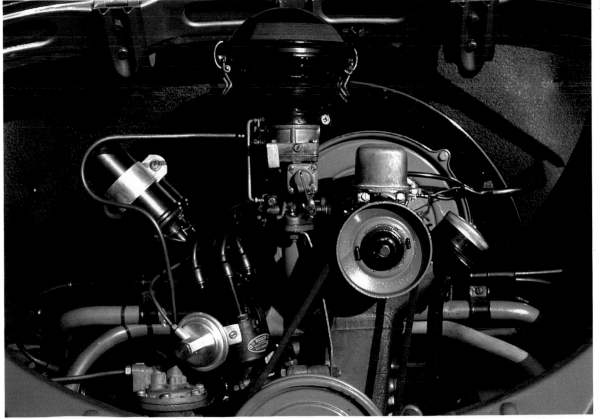

5

9

10

14

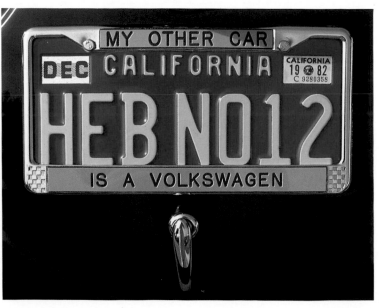

15

16

20

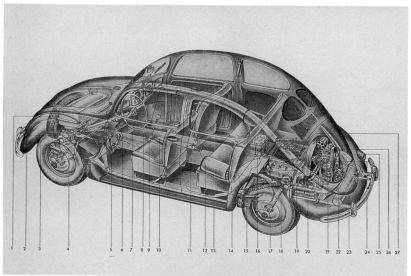

1 2 3 4 5 6 7 8 9 10 11 12 13 14 15 16 17 18 19 20 21 22 23 24 25 26 27

21

Drivers Controls

Are you familiar with the controls and instruments of your new VOLKS-WAGEN? Just take a seat behind the wheel, make yourself comfortable, and get acquainted first with all the various levers, switches, and controls. Some of the features are familiar to you already, but here are the full details:

INSTRUMENTS:

Speedometer	3
Control Light — Blue — Headlight Long Beam	1
Control Light — Red — Direction Indicator	2
Control Light — Red — Generator and Cooling System	5
Control Light — Green — Oil Pressure	4
Clock, 8-days Movement (Export Model)	6

FOOT CONTROLS:

Clutch Pedal	8
Brake Pedal	9
Accelerator Pedal	10
Headlight Beam Switch	7

HAND CONTROLS:

Steering Wheel	11
Gear Shift Lever	21
Hand Brake Lever	23
Ignition Switch	15
Starter Button	18
Signal Switch (Direction Indicator)	16
Switch for Windshield Wiper and Dome Lamp	14
Headlight Switch	17
Horn Button	12
Choke Control	24
Heater Control	20
Knob for Hood Lock	13
Knob for Winding and Setting the Clock (Export Model)	19
Fuel Shut-off Cock	25
Seat Adjusting Handle (Export Model)	22

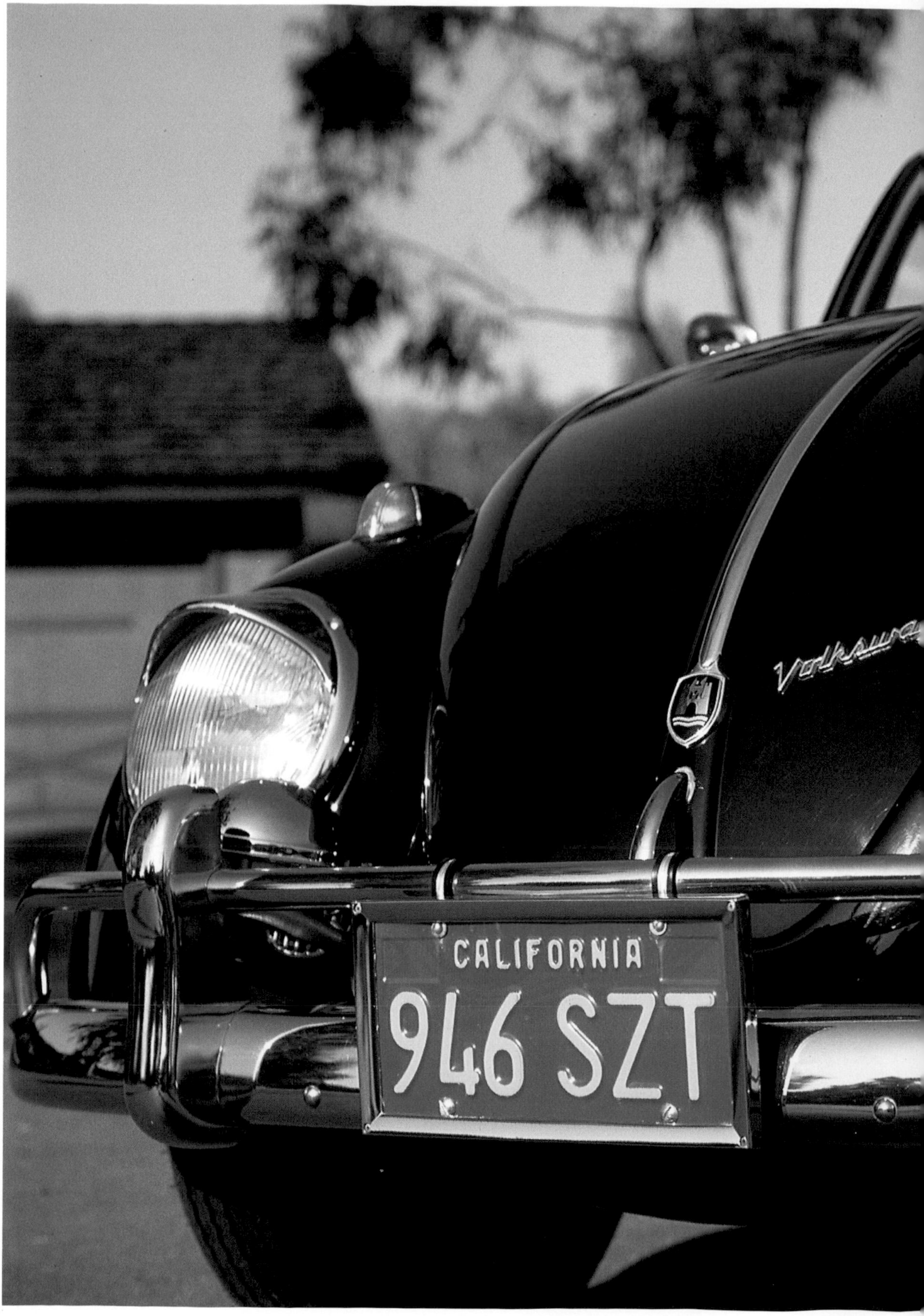
CALIFORNIA
946 SZT

25

26

27

28

29

32

33

36

37

38

Getting Ahead with
Volkswagen Trucks

Functional design

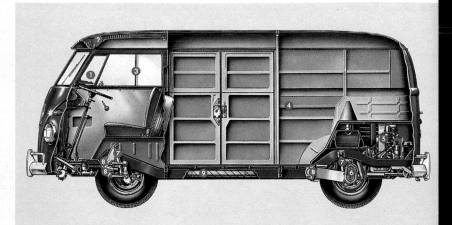

① Vent wings
② Special roof air-circulating system
③ Sliding windows

④ Loading compartment
⑤ Air-cooled Volkswagen engine
⑥ Reduction gear

⑦ Double-acting telescopic shock absorbers
⑧ Torsion bar suspension
⑨ Double-insulated warm-air heating system

41

SPECIFICATIONS

ENGINE

Type	4-cylinder, 4-stroke rear engine
Cyl. arrangement	2 pairs horizontally opposed
Valves	overhead type
Bore	3.031 in. (77 mm.)
Stroke	2.520 in. (64 mm.)
Displacement	72.740 cu. in. (1192 c.c.)
Compression ratio	6.6:1
Maximum b.h.p.	36 at 3700 r.p.m.
Piston speed	1427 ft./min. (7.25 m/s) at 3400 r.p.m. — 68 m.p.h. (110 km/h)
Lubrication	pressure lubrication (gear-type pump) with oil radiator
Oil capacity	5.3 U.S. pints (4.4 Imp. pints, 2.5 litres)
Fuel pump	Diaphragm type, mechanically operated
Carburetor	Downdraft carburetor with acceleration pump (Solex 28 PCI)
Air cleaner	Oil bath type
Cooling system	Air cooling by fan automatically controlled by thermostat
Battery	6 Volts, 66 a.h.
Starter	Solenoid type, Bosch make
Dynamo	Bosch, 160 watts, with voltage control

CLUTCH

Single disc, dry

TRANSMISSION

4 forward speeds, 1 reverse
De Luxe Model and Convertible
Controlled synchromesh on 2nd, 3rd and 4th gears

Gear ratios			
1st	3.60:1	2nd	1.88:1
3rd	1.23:1	4th	0.82:1
Reverse 4.63:1			

Standard Model
3rd and 4th gears silent

Gear ratios			
1st	3.60:1	2nd	2.07:1
3rd	1.25:1	4th	0.80:1
Reverse 6.60:1			

FINAL DRIVE

Power transmitted through spiral bevel gear, two-pinion bevel differential gear and swing axle shafts to rear wheels

Gear ratio	4.4:1
Oil capacity	of transmission and final drive: 3.3 U.S. pints (4.4 Imp. pints, 2.5 litres) Refill quantity 4.2 U.S. pints (3.5 Imp. pints, 2 litres)

CHASSIS

Frame	Tubular center section forked at rear and welded-on platform
Front axle	Independent suspension of wheels through upper and lower trailing arms; 2 transverse torsion bars protected in tubes
Rear axle	Independent suspension of wheels through swing axle shafts with trailing arms, one torsion bar on each side, mounted and protected in transverse tube
Shock absorbers	Front and rear: double-acting hydraulic telescopic type, requiring no maintenance
Steering	Special worm-type gear and divided track rod; 2.4 turns of steering wheel from lock to lock
Turning circle	approx. 36 ft.
Tires	5.60—15
Wheels	Disc type with drop-center rim 4 J × 15
Brakes	De Luxe Model and Convertible Hydraulic foot-brake (Lockheed) operating on four wheels; mechanical hand-brake operating on rear wheels Standard Model Mechanical foot and hand-brakes operating on four wheels
Wheelbase	94.5 in.
Track	Front 50.6 in. Rear 49.2 in.
Fuel tank capacity	10.6 U.S. gal. (8.75 Imp. gal., 40 liters) including 1.3 U.S. gal. (1.1 Imp. gal., 5 liters) reserve

OVERALL DIMENSIONS

Length:	160.2 in. (4070 mm.)
Width:	60.6 in. (1540 mm.)
Height:	59.1 in. (1500 mm.)

WEIGHTS in lbs. (kg)

	Sedan		Convertible	
Net weight	1565	(710)	1720	(780)
Unladen weight	1609	(730)	1763	(800)
Maximum load	838	(380)	794	(360)
Perm. total weight	2447	(1110)	2557	(1160)

PERFORMANCE

Fuel consumption	30 m.p.g. (Imp.), 32 m.p.g. (U.S.), 7.5 l/100 km
Max. and cruising speed	68 m.p.h. — 110 km/h
Climbing ability	1st gear 20.5° (37%) 2nd gear 10.5° (18.5%) 3rd gear 6.3° (11%) 4th gear 2.3° (4%)

Further Details: Radio and antenna are optional and are supplied as extra cost
Twin-good all-steel body with high-gloss weatherproof synthetic resin finish. Sound-proofing of partition between interior of car and engine compartment; twin exhaust muffler. Pleasing interior appointments; waist-line moulding on both sides of interior; recessed ashtray for rear seats; pocket in off-side door (De Luxe model); interior light with integral switch, also operated by door switches; rubber mats. Spacious luggage compartments behind rear seat and under front hood.

VOLKSWAGENWERK GMBH · WOLFSBURG
GERMANY

SEDAN
STANDARD AND DE LUXE MODELS

The Volkswagen Sedan is built in two models, Standard and De Luxe. They offer the same basic features which have made Volkswagens so outstandingly popular throughout the world. Both Standard and De Luxe look extremely attractive in their brilliant metallic finish. The De Luxe, in addition, offers a wide range of pleasing colors. Expensive upholstery and smart practical fittings form a stylish unit.

All Volkswagen models have surprisingly fast get-away and smooth, safe riding qualities due to their superbly designed suspension and low center of gravity. Combined with extraordinary economy and great comfort, these characteristic Volkswagen features make the cars unsurpassed in their class.

SUN ROOF

What a pleasant surprise! ... With only one hand you can easily fold back the top and breathe the fresh air and sunshine. With the Sun Roof closed, your car is as weatherproof as if it had a steel top.

CONVERTIBLE

Most critical among motorists are those who look for sports performance in a car open to wind and sun ... who are hard to please on the technical side and have their own ideas about comfort ... who want a car that is different from others and will reflect their own individuality. For these connoisseurs among motorists the Volkswagen Convertible is the perfect choice. No matter where it appears, it commands attention and arouses the admiration of everybody—indeed, could ever a lady's mind resist the beauty of its styling, the grace of its flowing lines and its ease of handling?

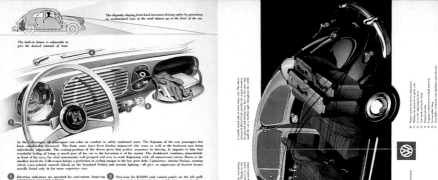

The elegantly sloping front hood increases driving safety by permitting an unobstructed view of the road almost up to the front of the car.

The built-in heater is adjustable to give the desired amount of heat.

In the Volkswagen all passengers can relax in comfort in softly cushioned seats. The legroom of the rear passengers has been considerably increased. The front seats have been further improved—the seats as well as the backrests now being individually adjustable. The seating-position of the driver gives him perfect assurance in driving. It imparts to him that wonderful feeling of being as much part of his car as the horseman is of his mount. The dashboard combines, immediately in front of his eyes, the vital instruments well grouped and easy to read, dispensing with all unnecessary extras. Down to the smallest detail the Volkswagen brings a perfection in styling unique in the low price field. Upholstery, interior fittings, steering wheel, ivory-colored controls (black on the Standard Sedan) and interior lighting—all give an impression of discreet luxury usually found only in far more expensive cars.

1. Direction indicators are operated by convenient, finger-tip STEERING COLUMN LEVER.

2. Large COMBINED INSTRUMENT UNIT contains speedometer with kilometer or mileage recorder and various warning lights attractively incorporated in the dial: red for dynamo and cooling system, green for oil pressure, blue for main beam, and a twin arrow for direction indicators.

3. Stylish light-colored, easy-to-grip TWIN SPOKE STEERING WHEEL with horn button featuring the emblem of the Volkswagen town.

4. WINDSHIELD WIPER. De Luxe models are fitted with more powerful, self-parking wipers.

5. Provision for RADIO and control panel; on the left, pull-push switches for headlights, windshield wipers, and adjustment of speedometer light.

6. Ample room for installation of LOUDSPEAKER behind the decorative grille.

7. Pull-out CHOKE CONTROL to assist starting, conveniently placed on right of instrument panel.

8. Combined IGNITION and STARTING SWITCH. Ignition key also locks driver's door.

9. Large, hinged ASH TRAY.

10. Roomy, lockable GLOVE COMPARTMENT.

Park it with a smile! Volkswagens are so compact and maneuverable that you can usually find a space large enough to get into easily.

49   50

Drivers and passengers are seated in the best-sprung part of the vehicle, between the axles. Thanks to this design, which is set well on independent springing, even if one negotiates an expanse of rolling comfort which is usually found only in much larger cars. The absence of any rear-axle humps provides the utmost comfort. In the interior all the controls fall readily under the driver's hands so that one made the car a familiar sight throughout the world.

1. Luggage compartment under front hood
2. Steering column lever operating direction indicators
3. Lever for operating fuel tap
4. Pedal assembly
5. Gear shift and hand-brake lever
6. Defroster vent
7. Ventilation wings with inside catch
8. Arm-rest
9. Heater outlet

10. Rotary switch for heater adjustment
11. Starting control for pool fuel
12. Lever for adjusting backrest
13. Seat back adjustment strap
14. Shaped ash-tray
15. Luggage compartment behind rear seat
16. Lever-glide lining
17. Head-lights combined with fuel-filler and indicators

AIR COOLING SYSTEM

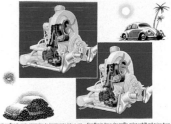

Sure, air-cooling is more expensive to incorporate into a car but we feel that Volkswagen owners are entitled to enjoy the full advantages of such an advanced design. Don't worry, neither tropical heat nor arctic cold can do the engine any harm. Under toughest conditions it will jump to action on the turn of the starter and purr along contentedly for miles on end, as matter where you drive. It will scamper up the steepest mountain like a hound on the heels of a jack rabbit.

Crawling in dense city traffic, going uphill and going down ... Volkswagen engines are kept at the proper temperature, automatically controlled by a thermostat which opens or throttles the passage of the air flow according to prevailing conditions. Indeed, air-cooling eliminates dozens of troubles inherent in water-cooling systems. It is largely due to this system that so many Volkswagen owners have already been driving 150,000 miles with the same engine—and they would never think of having another make.

TRANSMISSION

The sturdy four-speed transmission has synchronized second, third and fourth gears. Its high degree of flexibility makes the Volkswagen master of any situation that may arise in city or country driving. In first gear it can climb a 37% grade and you will not easily find a road which is as steep as that.

CARBURETOR

The Volkswagen carburetor, the most advanced type of downdraft carburetor ever made, is equipped with an acceleration pump. Its well-designed features insure fast acceleration and smoother flow of power with low fuel consumption. All these advantages contribute to the remarkable overall performance of the Volkswagen.

51   52

53

54

59

61

62

63

67

68

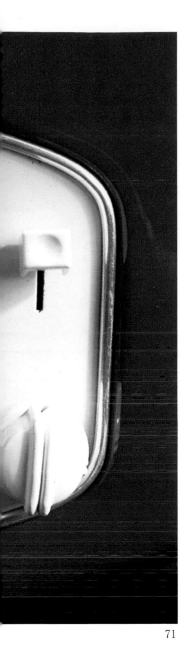

73

74

71

75

76

77

82

83

86

87

The Volkswagen Transporters

The Volkswagen Range of Micro Buses

The transporter models equipped for the carriage of passengers, including the VW Kombi, are available – as requested – with seating for 7 or 8 persons. In the seven-seater versions the driver's bench and the forward bench of the passenger compartment are made to seat two persons.

91

92

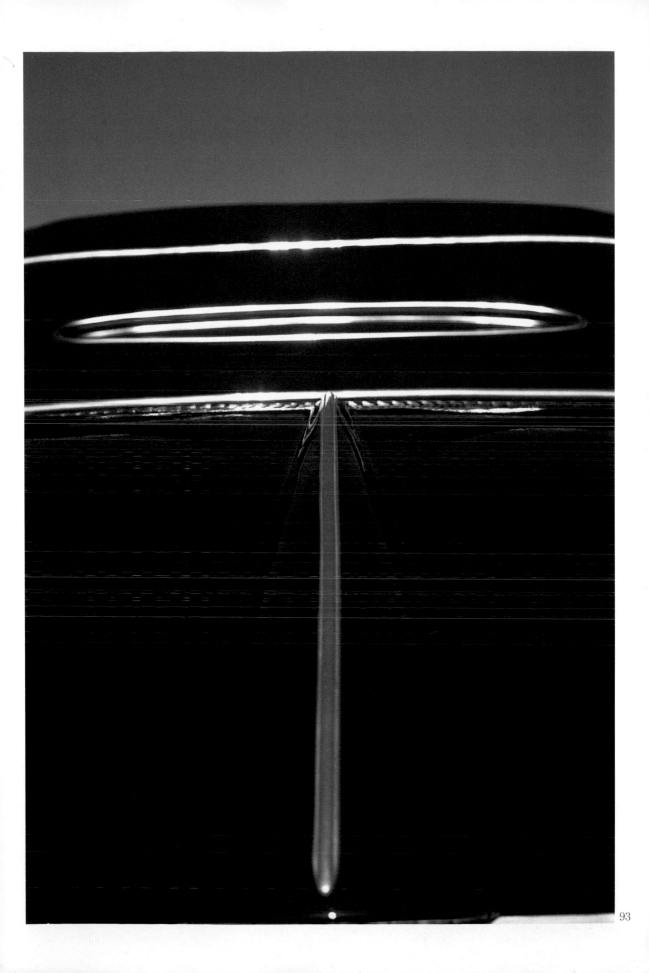

96

97

98

101

102

OLD VOLKSWAGENS NEVER DIE··········

DESCRIPTION

① 1957 TypeⅠ OVAL-WINDOW, RUG-TOP
   CHASSIS NUMBER : 1 426 709
   BODY COLOR : POLAR SILVER
   OWNER : RICH KIMBALL／TUSTIN, CA
② Front-hood open── Spare wheel and gas tank in sight.
③ Dashboard ── Panel for accessories
   (This panel was optional in the 1950s).
④ Dashboard through Oval-window.
⑤ Original Engine ── Beautiful forever.
⑥ 1959 Type Ⅰ CONVERTIBLE
   CHASSIS NUMBER : 2 299 475
   BODY COLOR : RUBY RED (TOP＝IVORY)
   OWNER : RICH KIMBALL／TUSTIN, CA

⑦ Left Side.
⑧ Right Side.
⑨ 1951 Type Ⅰ SPLIT-WINDOW
   CHASSIS NUMBER : 1 317 695
   BODY COLOR : BLACK
   OWNER : RICH KIMBALL／TUSTIN, CA
⑨ Semaphore with vintage VW only──VW logo
   can be seen in the center of plastic plate.
⑩ Rear view

⑪ 1952 TypeⅠ SPLIT-WINDOW
   CHASSIS NUMBER : 1 374 768
   BODY COLOR : IVORY
   OWNER : ALBERT BIEHL／FRESNO, CA
⑫ 1952 Type Ⅰ SPLIT-WINDOW
   CHASSIS NUMBER : 1 291 466
   BODY COLOR : DARK BLUE
   OWNER : ALBERT BIEHL／FRESNO, CA

⑬ 1949 HEBMULLER
   CHASSIS NUMBER : 1 102 364
   BODY COLOR : CHOCOLATE BROWN & BROWN (TOP＝IVORY)
   OWNER : MAUREY COLE／HUNTINGTON BEACH, CA
⑭ Dashboard of Hebmuller.
⑮ THe 12th model by Hebmuller──It is
   indicated on the license plate.
⑯ Engine with OKRASA tuning kit
   installed.
⑰ The most beautiful angle for Hebmuller.
⑱ 1952 Type Ⅰ SPLIT-WINDOW
   CHASSIS NUMBER : 1 386 935
   BODY COLOR : OLIVE GREEN
   OWNER : HIROSHI HAYAKAWA／NAGOYA, JAPAN
⑲ Rear view.
⑳ Dashboard through Split-window.
㉑㉓ Instruction manual for 1951 beetle.
㉒ Dashboard ── Nostalgic atmosphere of
   Vintage VWs is fascinating

㉔ 1960 Type Ⅰ PROTOTYPE OF A／T, RUG-TOP
   CHASSIS NUMBER : 3 360 241

BODY COLOR : BLACK
OWNER : W.K. & MARY LEADLEY∕LA MESA, CA

㉕ Prototype of 1960 beetle with automatic
transmission. Automatic model was first put on the market in 1968.
Apparently, VW had been undergoing several
tests for automatics for long before 1968.

㉖ Automatic transmission——Gear change lever.

㉗ Auxiliary one-gallon tank (Not genuine VW accessory).

㉘ Stone guard for Rear fender.

㉙ Original Engine.

㉚ Blue-sky and landscape is beautifully
reflected on the black body.

㉛ 1951 Type I SPLIT-WINDOW, RUG-TOP
CHASSIS NUMBER : 1 212 043
BODY COLOR : MEDIUM BLUE
OWNER : FLAT4 CO., LTD. TOKYO, JAPAN

㉜ Dashboard —— glovebox with door, flower vase,
Telefunken radio, etc.

㉝ Rear view.

㉞ Ventilation flap was installed with 1951
model only.

㉟ 1959 Type II DELIVERY VAN
CHASSIS NUMBER . 487031
BODY COLOR : GRAY
OWNER : BOB SCOTT∕GLENDALE, CA

㊱ VW Type II pioneered 1-box car which is
quite useful for business and leisure, as well.

㊲ VW logo symbolizes Type II.

㊳ Front turn signal.

㊴㊵ Sales catalog for 1958～1959 model
with colorful illustrations.

㊶ 1955 Type I CONVERTIBLE
CHASSIS NUMBER : 1 761 681
BODY COLOR : BLACK (TOP＝BLACK)
OWNER : TONY MOORE∕WHITTIER, CA

㊷ Convertible in excellent condition.
Black and red are beautifully contrasted.

㊸ Part of Rear.

㊹ Petrol burning heater —— optional parts in the 1950s.

㊺～㊿ Sales catalog for 1954 model.
This catalog is also a collector's item.

㊼ 1956 Type I OVAL-WINDOW
CHASSIS NUMBER : 1 371 421
BODY COLOR : SILVER METALLIC
OWNER : JACK GHAN∕ARCADIA, CA

㊽ 1953 Type I OVAL-WINDOW
CHASSIS NUMBER : 1 463 826
BODY COLOR : BLACK
OWNER : RANDY MASKELL∕BURBANK, CA

㊾ Palm tree grown on top of a beetle ?!

㊿ Left side.

Dr. Porsche, who designed this lovely line, is great.

57 1957 Type I CONVERTIBLE
CHASSIS NUMBER : 1 402 438
BODY COLOR : SAND BAIGE (TOP＝BLACK)
OWNER : BOB SCOTT／GLENDALE, CA

58 Rear view.
The color of this car is comparatively rare.

59 1957 Convertible with top down.

60 1958 KARMANN-GHIA CONVERTIBLE
CHASSIS NUMBER : 1 951 695
BODY COLOR : BLUE GRAY(TOP＝IVORY)
OWNER : FLAT4 CO., LTD. TOKYO, JAPAN

61 Highly refined dashboard.

62 Badge of Karmann.

63 Beautiful Emblem.

64 Air-Intake with two crome lines was installed
for vintage Karmann only.

65 The elegant body line of Karmann-Ghia
fascinates many VW fans.

66 1958 ROMETSCH
CHASSIS NUMBER : 1 741 493
BODY COLOR : IVORY & BLACK (TOP＝BLACK)
OWNER : PHIL & MARY LEADLEY／TUSTIN, CA

67 69 Rometsch is an extremely rare two-seater
sports car.
We are quite happy that we could photograph
it for this book.

68 Dashboard resembles a Porsche Speedstar.

70 1949 HEBMULLER
CHASSIS NUMBER : 1 126 410
BODY COLOR : RUBY RED & IVORY (TOP＝DARK GREY)
OWNER : BOB GILMORE／SAN DIEGO, CA

71 Driving VW with good music is a lot of fun.

72 Dashboard.

73 Badge of Hembuller.

74 Special badge given to every VW owner
who registered 100,000Km.

75 Speedmeter.

76 1961 Type I CONVERTIBLE
CHASSIS NUMBER : 3 206 950
BODY COLOR : TURQUOISE GREEN (TOP＝BLACK)
OWNER : KURT ROMELSBACHER／EL SEGUNDO, CA

77 One sunny afternoon in LA. It looks as if fragrance
of sweet oranges is wafting around.

78 1957 Type I OVAL-WINDOW
CHSSIS NUMBER : 1 573 914
BODY COLOR : HORIZON BLUE
OWNER : DREW SHRYOCK／PORTLAND, OREGON

80 1949 HEBMULLER
CHASSIS NUMBER : 1 126 411
BODY COLOR : BLACK & IVORY (TOP＝BLACK)

OWNER : FLAT4 CO., LTD. TOKYO, JAPAN
(81) All VW maniacs long for Hebmuller, six of which appear in this book.
(82) Back in the early 1950s dashboard was often decorated with flowers.
We wish we could afford to enjoy such luxury even today.
(83) Original Engine.
(84) Semaphore of Hebmuller pops up out of front quarter-panel.
(85) 1957 Type II MICRO BUS
CHASSIS NUMBER : 322738
BODY COLOR : SEALING WAX RED & CHESTNUT BROWN
OWNER : RICH KIMBALL／TUSTIN, CA
(86) Side view.
(87) Rear view.
(88)(89) Sales catalog for 1957 model.
It contains an illustration of VW in the same color as the car shown here.
(90) 1961 Type I CONVERTIBLE
CHASSIS NUMBER : 3 291 224
BODY COLOR : RUBY RED (TOP=BLACK)
OWNER : MIKE HORNBECKER／INGLEWOOD, CA

(91) 1949 HEBMULLER
CHASSIS NUMBER : 1 138 621
BODY COLOR : CHOCOLATE BROWN & IVORY (TOP=BLACK)
OWNER : W.K. & MARY BELCHER／INGLEWOOD, CA
(92) Left side.
(93) Artistic angle !
(94) 1949 HEBMULLER
CHASSIS NUMBER : 1 110 814
BODY COLOR : BROWN & IVORY (TOP=BLACK)
OWNER : STEVE HERRON／SANTA BARBRA, CA

(95) The picture on the page before was the horn of this car.
(96) Telefunken radio and Flower vase.
(97) Semaphore.
(98) Exhaust-pipe end with ornamentation.
(99) Top of Hebmuller can be completely encased inside its body.
(100) 1949 HEBMULLER
CHASSIS NUMBER : 1 195 386
BODY COLOR : CORAL RED & BLACK (TOP=BLACK)
OWNER : ALBERT BIEHL／FRESNO, CA

(101) Right side.
(102) Black and red — unique but original two-tone color.
(103) 1952 Type I SPLIT-WINDOW
CHASSIS NUMBER : 1 329 150
BODY COLOR : BLUE GRAY
OWNER : EIJI HIRAOKA／FUKUOKA, JAPAN

① The one-piece tail-light, used from 1954 until 1961.

② Heart tail-light, used from 1952 until 1954.

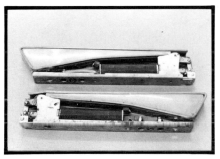

③ Semaphore for Vintage VW.

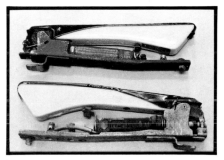

④ Semaphore for Vintage VW.

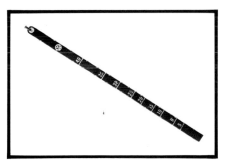

⑤ Unequipped with Fuel gauge on early VW, this device was used to measure petrol in the gas tank in those days.

⑥ The Wolfsburg badge fitted to the front hood of Beetles from 1951 to 1962. Left is earty type and right is late type.

VINTAGE VW PARTS

Since it was first born in 1938, Volkswagen beetle never changed its basic form duriug the forty years in production until they ceased to manufacture it any longer in West Germany. However, it is quite interesting to make a little study of the chronological changes and improvements undergone on various parts of VW every year. Now we will show you some of the accessories and the parts used in vintage beetles.

⑦ The round horn grille, used from July 1949 until the end of September 1952.

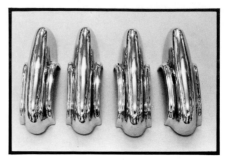

⑧ Bumper guard (early type).

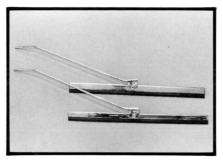

⑨ Windshield wipers (early type).

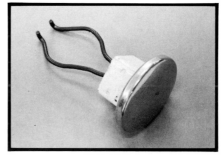

⑩ Exhaust end pipe.

⑪ Flower vase in porcelain (dark blue in\ colour) and its case.

⑫ Parts to cover the hole of Jack-Up Point. (It can be a tool to unscrew wheel cap as well.)

⑬ Gas-tank cap (early type).

⑭ Anti-dazzle vizor.

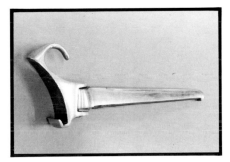

⑮ Coat-hunger for Type-II.

⑯ Headlight vizor (early type).

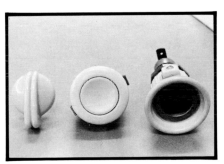

⑰ Headlight switch／Starter switch／
Cigar-liter. From Left.

⑱ Steering wheel of Karmann-ghia up to
1959.

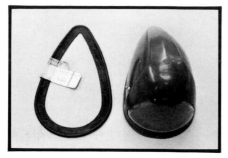

⑲ "Pope's Nose" license-plale light and gasket.

⑳ License-plate light and gasket.

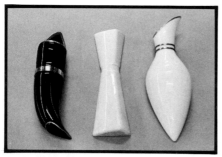

㉑ Of numerous sorts of Flower vases, these three were made of ceramics.

㉒ Turn-signal for U.S. model (1955〜1957).

㉓ The badge fitted to the frond quarter-panel of the Hebmuller.

㉔ Spare wheel hub cap with VW tools.

㉕ Gradual changes of steering wheel.   From Ⓐ to Ⓒ is chronological order.

㉖ Emblems fitted to Beetles
Ⓐ is early type with the logo yet unembossed. Ⓑ and Ⓒ carry the embossed logo.

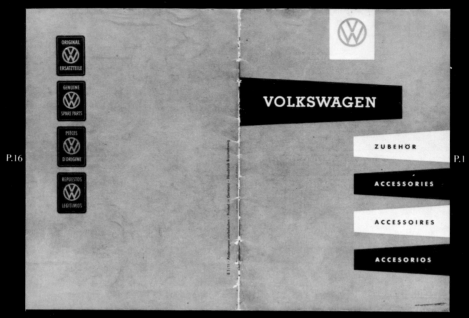

Back Cover   Front Cover

ABOVE／Seat-covers   CENTER／Radio receiving set with fittings including antenna (Telefunken Auto-Super)   BELOW／Net

VINTAGE VW ACCESSORY LITERATURE

There were excellent accessories and parts for Volkswagen beetles manufactured in the 1950s. Many of those parts can still work in good condition even today, because they were so good and strong. Refined to the utmost efficiency and parcticability, they afforded the owners of VW great pleasure to own it and drive it in those days. Fortunately, we can still enjoy the pleasure of driving VW even today. It is a very pleasant fact for all fans of VW.
Now, we are going to show you the accessories and parts catalog that VOLKSWAGEN in West Germany distributed to the owners of VW in 1955.

Kraftstoffvorratsanzeiger
Fuel gauge
Indicateur de niveau d'essence
Indicator de nivel de combustible
SP 75   für Volkswagen
SP 76   für Transporter
SP 76 a für Transporter März 1955

11 040 331
Ascher am Schalthebel
Ashtray on gear change lever
Cendrier sur levier des vitesses
Cenicero en la palanca del cambio

11 016 201 d
Zeituhr, elektrisch an Schalttafel
Clock, electric, Instrument panel
Montre electrique, de bord
Reloj eléctrico en tablero de mando

11 040 305
Blumenvase, Kristall
Flower vase, cut glas
Porte-bouquet, cristal
Florero, cristal

ABOVE/Fuel gauge
BELOW/Clock, electric,
      Instrument panel

ABOVE/Ashtrey on gear change lever
BELOW/Flower vase, cut glas

11 040 351
Hupenring Farbe: graubeige,
hellgrau, elfenbein
Horn ring colors: gray-beige,
light-grey, ivory
Anneau d'avertisseur, couleurs:
gris-beige, gris clair, ivoire
Anillo de bocina, Colores:
beige gris, gris claro, marfil

15 857 571 a
Haltegriff an Schalttafel
Grip —/Instrument panel
Poignée de retenue
(se fixant à la planche de bord)
Asidero en el tablero
de mando

11 019 051
Sonnenschutzblende Plexiglas
Sunshade easily
Ecrans pare-soleil
Parasol de plexiglas

11 019 025
Gepäckträger mit Holzroste für
geschlossenen Volkswagen / momeno
Luggage rail with wooden grid for
Volkswagen
Porte-bagages (fond à clairevoie en
bois pour conduites intérieures)
Porta equipajes con rejilla de ma-
Parasol (lado derecho)

11 019 025 a
für Volkswagen mit Schiebedach
for Volkswagen with sliding roof
pour conduites intérieures
toit ouvrant
para Coches del Turismo VW
techo corredizo

211 019 025
Gepäckträger mit Holzroste für
Transporter, Größe 200 × 125 cm
Luggage rail with wooden grid for
Transporters, Size: 200 × 125 cm
Porte-bagages (fond à clairevoie
en bois par véhicules utilitaires)
200 × 125 cm
Porta equipajes con rejilla de ma-
dera para Vehiculos de Transpo-
porte VW 200 × 125 cm

241 019 025
für Transporter mit Schiebedach,
Größe: 120 × 125 cm
for Transporters with sliding roof,
size: 120 × 125 cm
pour véhicules utilitaires toit
ouvrant 120 × 125 cm
para Vehiculos de Transporte VW
con techo corredizo 120 × 125 cm

ABOVE/Horn ring colors : gray-beige,
      light-gray, ivory
CENTER/Grip-Instrument panel
BELOW/Sunshade easily

ABOVE/Luggage rail with wooden grid for
      Volkswagen
BELOW/Luggage rail with wooden grip for
      Transporters.

11 019 075
Sonnenblende mit Rückblickspiegel, doppelseitig
Rear view mirror with anti-dazzle vizor
Pare-soleil double avec rétroviseur
Parasoles en ambos con retrovisor

11 019 081
Sonnenblende für rechte Seite
Anti-dazzle vizor, right side
Para-soleil, côté droit
Parasol (lado derecho)

11 040 231
Scheibenwaschanlage
mit Zugpumpe
Windshield washer
with pressure pump
Laveur de pare-brise, avec pompe
Lavador de parabrisas con bomba
de presión

11 040 181
Rückblickspiegel,
Befestigung am Türscharnier
Rear view mirror, mounted on door hinge
Rétroviseur tà fixer à la
charnière de la porte)
Espejo retrovisor (fijación a la
bisagra de la puerta)

11 019 041
Koffersatz:
3 Koffer für Kofferraum hinten
1 Koffer für Kofferraum vorn

Set of suitcases:
3 suitcases for rear luggage compartment
1 suitcases for front luggage compartment

Série de valises comprenant:
un ensemble de 3 valises s'adaptant dans
le compartiment à bagages arrières
une valises se plaçant dans le compartiment
à bagages avant

Juego de maletas para Coches de Turismo VW:
3 maletas para compartimiento de
equipaje trasero
1 maleta para compartimiento de
equipaje delantero

11 040 183
Rückblickspiegel, Befestigung
am Türrahmen
Rear view mirror, mounted on door frame
Rétroviseur tà fixer à l'encadrement
de la porte)
Espejo retrovisor (fijación a la
puerta) al marco

ABOVE① / Rear view mirror
ABOVE② / Anti-dazzle vizor, right side
CENTER / Rear view mirror, mounted on
    door hinge
BELOW / Rear view mirror, mounted on door frame

ABOVE / Windshield washer with pressure pump
BELOW / Set of suitcases (3 suitcases for rear
    luggage compartment / 1 suitcases for
    front luggage compartment)

11 040 101
Blendenring für Scheibenrad, glatt
Road wheel ornamental ring, plain
Couronne de roue (non ajourée)
Corona de rueda lisa

15 040 149
Schutz-Ecken für hintere Kotflügel
Rear fender protection
Plaque de protection de bas d'aile
Placas de protección para
guardabarros traseros

15 040 163
Auspuffhülse, verchromt
Exhaust end pipe,
chromium plated
Embout d'échappement
(chromée)
Tubo de escape cromado

11 040 103
Blendenring für Scheibenrad, getächert
Road wheel ornamental ring, fan-shaped
Couronne de roue (ajourée)
Corona de rueda calada

11 012 641
Schneekette für Volkswagen 5.60 × 15
feingliedrige, verschleißfeste Spezial-Gleitschutzkette
Snow chain for Volkswagen 5.60 × 15
special small-link corrosion resistant anti-skid chain
Chaîne anti-déparante pour voitures 5.60 × 15
(maillons fins spéciaux résistant à l'usure)
Cadena antideslizante para coches de Turismo VW 5.60 × 15
(eslabones finos, resistentes al des gaste)

211 012 641
Schneekette für Transporter 5.50 × 16
feingliedrige, verschleißfeste Spezial-Gleitschutzkette
Snow chain to transporters 5.50 × 16
special small-link corrosion resistant anti-skid chain
Chaîne anti-déparante pour utilitaires 5.50 × 16
(maillons fins spéciaux résistant à l'usure)
Cadena antideslizante para Vehículos
de Transporte VW 5.50 × 16
(eslabones finos, resistentes al desgaste)

11 601 155
Zierring für Scheibenrad
Road wheel ornamental ring
Cercle chromé de roue
Anillo de adorno para rueda
de disco, cromado

ABOVE / Road wheel ornamental ring, plain
CENTER / Road wheel ornamental ring,
    fan-shaped
BELOW / Road wheel ornamental ring

ABOVE / Rear fender protection
CENTER / Exhaust end pipe, chromium plated
BELOW / Snow chain for Volkswagen 5.60 × 15

11 040 211
Such-Scheinwerfer
Spot light
Projecteur orientable
Proyector orientable

Konservierungsmittel
Preservative for synthetic
resin lacquer
Produit d'entretien pour laques
synthétiques
Conservante
L 190   = 1,0 kg
L 190.5 = 0,5 kg

Polierwasser
Polishing fluid
Liquide de lustrage
Agua de pulimento
L 170   = 1,0 kg
L 170.5 = 0,5 kg

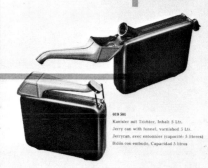

095 038
Nebel-Scheinwerfer 110 mm ⌀
Fog lamp 110 mm. dia.
Phare antibrouillard 110 mm ⌀
Faro de niebla 110 mm ⌀

095 033
Rückfahr-Scheinwerfer
Reversing light
Projecteur de recul
Faro de marcha atrás

019 501
Kanister mit Trichter, Inhalt 5 Ltr.
Jerry can with funnel, varnished 5 Ltr.
Jerrycan, avec entonnoir (capacité: 5 litres)
Bidón con embudo, Capacidad 5 litros

ABOVE / Spot light
CENTER / Fog lamp 110mm. dia.
BELOW / Reversing light

ABOVE / Preservative for synthetic resin laqcuer
BELOW / Jerry can with funnel, varnished 5 Ltr.

11 012 025 b
Werkzeug
im Radkappen-Behälter
Spare wheel hub cap with
tools
Boîte à outils (se logeant
dans la roue de secours)
Herramientas en la rueda
de recambio

1Z 300
Werkzeugsatz, Chrom-Vanadium
Set of Automotive tool for
Volkswagen, chrome-vanadium
Jeux d'outil, Acier au
chrome-Vanadium
Juego de herramientas.
acero al cromo-vanadio

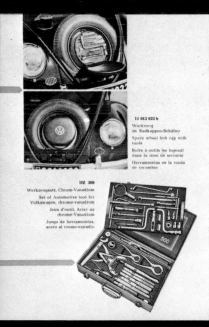

VW 1001
Werkzeugsatz, Chrom-Vanadium
Set of Automotive tool for Volkswagen,
chrome-vanadium
Jeux d'outil, Acier au chromé-
Vanadium
Juego de herramientas, acero al cromo-
vanadio

VW 1100
Werkzeugwagen-Assistent, Chrom-
Vanadium
Tool trolley — Assistent with VW
tool set, chromo vanadium
Chariot à outils — Assistent, Acier
au chromé-Vanadium
Carretilla de herramientas Assistent,
acero al cromo-vanadio

ABOVE / Spare wheel hub cap with tools
BELOW / Set of Automotive tool for
Volkswagen, chrome-vanadium

ABOVE / Set of Automotive tool for Volkswagen,
chrome-vanadium
BELOW / Tool trolley-Assistant with VW tool set,
chrome-vanadium

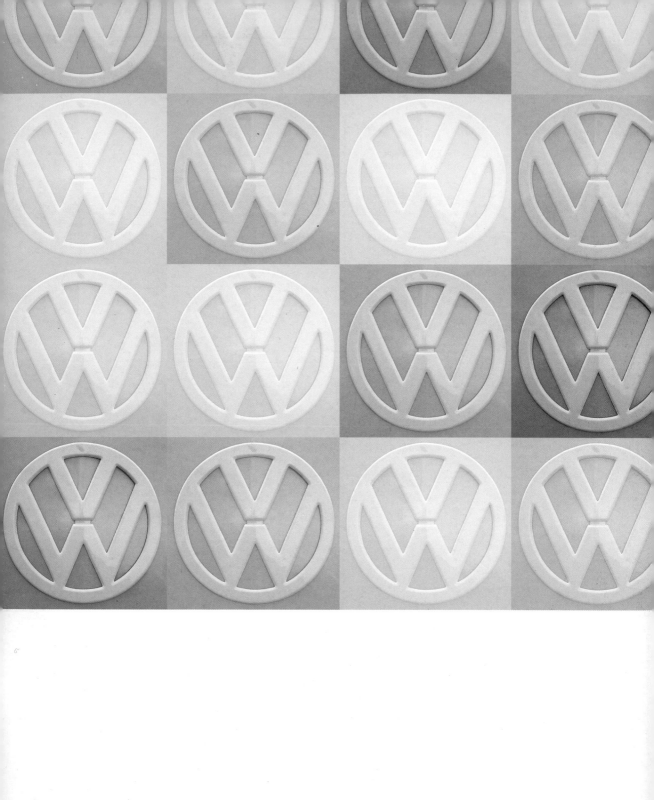